France *1700–1800*

William Rieder

Philadelphia Museum of Art

Cover: Writing Table, 1783, by
Jean-Henri Riesener (*see* page 26)

Photography by Will Brown

Printing by Lebanon Valley Offset

Box 7646, Philadelphia, Pa. 19101

Library of Congress Cataloging in Publication Data

Rieder, William.
France, 1700-1800.

(Guides to European decorative arts; no. 3)
Bibliography: p.
1. Decorative arts—France—History—18th century—Catalogs. 2. Decorative arts—Pennsylvania—Philadelphia—Catalogs. 3. Philadelphia Museum of Art—Catalogs. I. Philadelphia Museum of Art. II. Title. III. Series.
NK947.R53 1983 745′.0944′0740148ll 83-6230
ISBN 0-87633-052-9

Introduction

The decorative arts were brought to an extraordinary level of refinement and sophistication in France during the eighteenth century. This achievement can be fully seen in the Philadelphia Museum of Art, principally through the generosity of one benefactor, Mrs. Alexander Hamilton Rice. In 1939 Mrs. Rice bequeathed to the Museum the contents of the drawing room of her house at 901 Fifth Avenue in New York, which contained one of the finest collections of French furniture and decorative arts in the country. Born Eleanore Elkins, the daughter of one of the Museum's great benefactors, George W. Elkins, she was surrounded from childhood by great works of art of many different periods. Her first husband, George B. Widener, and their son Harry, a distinguished bibliophile, were lost on the *Titanic;* some years later she married the geographer and explorer Dr. Alexander Hamilton Rice.

In 1912 Mrs. Rice met the great art dealer Joseph Duveen, who soon became her friend and advisor, helping her assemble a large collection of old master paintings and sculpture, carpets, tapestries, French and Chinese ceramics, and French furniture—almost all from his own firm—with which she furnished houses in New York, Newport, and Paris. Her collecting interests increasingly focused on French eighteenth-century decorative arts, the best of which were in her New York drawing room, which has been recreated at the Museum.

A friend who shared Mrs. Rice's interest in the eighteenth century was Fiske Kimball, director of the Philadelphia Museum of Art from 1924 to 1954. In 1928, with his encouragement, she gave the Museum an important Louis XVI room, the salon from the Hôtel Letellier in Paris. With this gift and her subsequent bequest of the furnishings of her drawing room, she enriched the Museum with objects of great beauty and rarity.

Table, c. 1770
Martin Carlin (*maître* 1766, died 1785)

6 Martin Carlin was one of the leading Parisian cabinetmakers of the second half of the eighteenth century. The high quality of his craftsmanship brought him important patrons, and a considerable quantity of his furniture was produced for the Crown. He is perhaps best known for small, portable, and very refined tables, which he made in several types. This oblong table has three graduated tiers, the largest at bottom, held in place by four fluted pilasters, which continue into cabriole legs. The marquetry patterns of the top (interlaced quatrefoils with floral centers) and the two lower tiers (a stylized oak leaf surrounded by a band of radiating tulipwood) recur on a number of tables and upright cabinets by Carlin. The gilt-bronze gallery included on each tier and the mounts on the feet and knees of the legs were also used repeatedly by Carlin.

In the late nineteenth century this table belonged to the Marquis of Headfort; it passed to his daughter, Lady Olivia Fitz-Patrick, and granddaughter, Mrs. Cornwallis West. The table was acquired from her by Duveen and sold to Mrs. Rice.

Oak veneered with rosewood, tulipwood, boxwood, and sycamore; gilt-bronze mounts
Stamp: M CARLIN (indistinct) with the monogram of the Guild, JME (under bottom tier)
Height $31\frac{13}{16}''$ (81 cm), width $26\frac{3}{4}''$ (68 cm), depth $17\frac{1}{4}''$ (44 cm)
Bequest of Eleanore Elkins Rice. 39-41-12

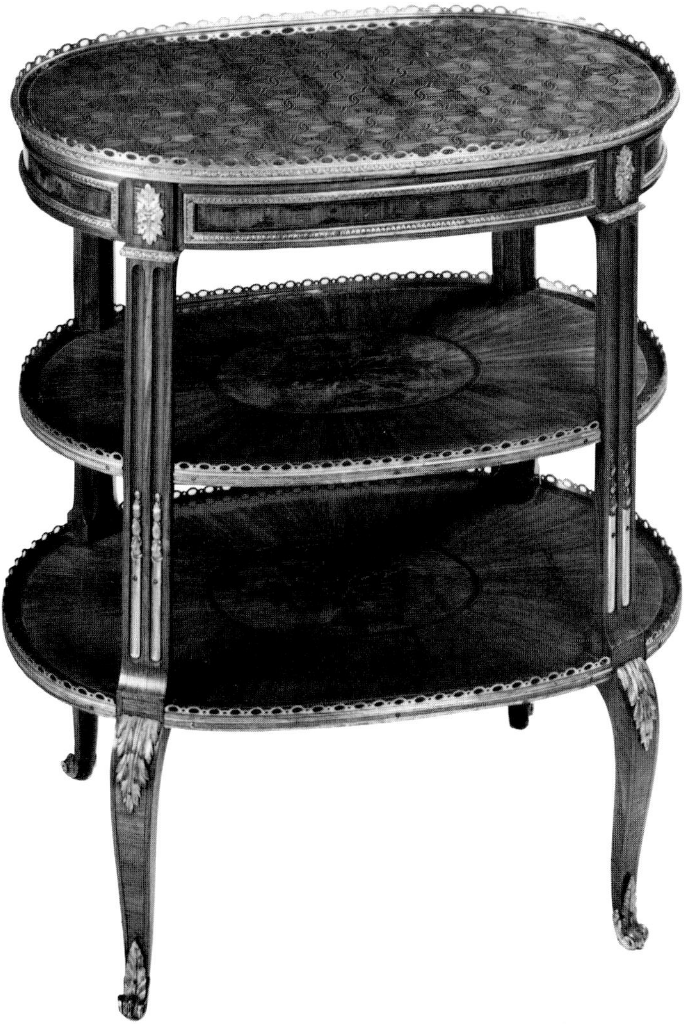

Writing Table, c. 1770
Martin Carlin (*maître* 1766, died 1785)

8 This type of small writing table with a raised cabinet at back containing drawers or a shelf, sometimes closed by doors or a tambour shutter, is known as a *bonheur-du-jour.* The earliest use of this term, for which there is no English equivalent, dates to 1770, and the form continued to be popular until the Revolution. Pairs of *bonheurs-du-jour* are rare, and even rarer are pairs veneered with positive and negative marquetry—such as this and its mate in the Museum—where the foreground wood in the ornamental panels on one table is reversed to form the background in the panels on the other. Both tables have a large central drawer fitted identically with a writing panel hinged at back and with compartments for writing materials at right. The tables are veneered in rosewood, sycamore, holly, and ebony, with a trellis pattern enclosing a quatrefoil, a design repeated by Carlin with variations on a number of commodes, night tables, and traveling tables. The backs of these two tables are inlaid with a trellis pattern with dots of ebony at the intersections, a motif used also by the cabinetmakers Adam Weisweiler, Jean-Henri Riesener, and Bernard Molitor. The gilt-bronze corner mount of a satyr mask with oak-leaf spray is found also on a group of contemporaneous Sèvres-mounted jewel caskets attributed to Carlin (three in the Metropolitan Museum of Art, New York).

J. Pierpont Morgan acquired these tables separately in 1905 from Duveen and Jacques Seligmann, thereby re-uniting the pair. They were exhibited with the Morgan collection at the Metropolitan Museum of Art in 1914, acquired by Duveen, and sold the following year to Mrs. Rice.

Oak veneered with rosewood, sycamore, holly, and ebony; gilt-bronze mounts
Stamp: M CARLIN with the monogram of the Guild, JME (beneath left and right rail)
Height $31\frac{7}{8}$″ (81 cm), width $21\frac{5}{8}$″ (55 cm), depth $14\frac{9}{16}$″ (37 cm)
Bequest of Eleanore Elkins Rice
39-41-11a

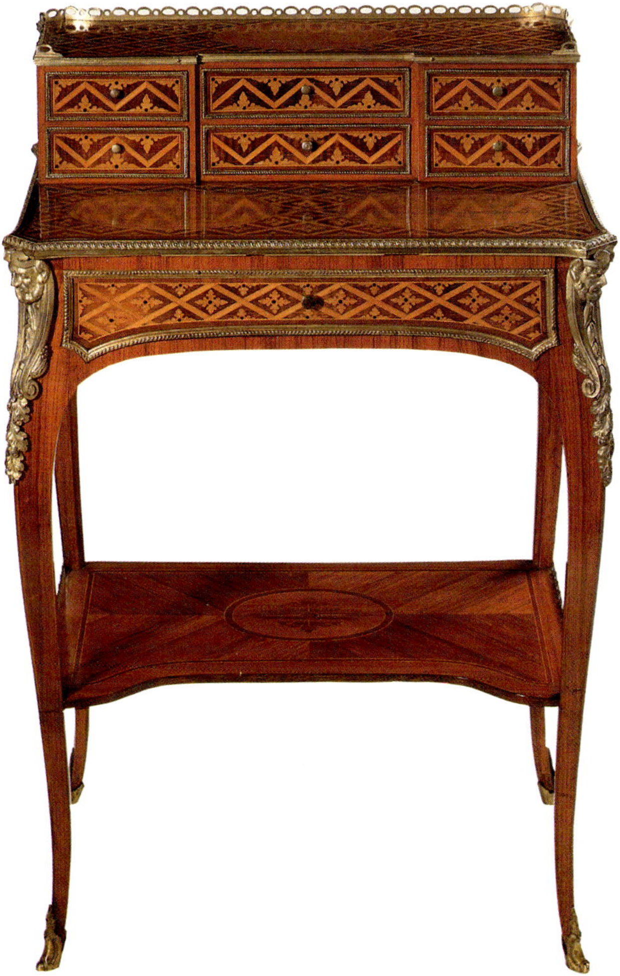

Writing Table, c. 1777–80
Martin Carlin (*maître* 1766, died 1785)

10

This *bonheur-du-jour* is mounted with fifteen Sèvres porcelain plaques painted with pink roses on a white ground and with borders of turquoise blue (a color known in the eighteenth century as *bleu céleste*). The plaques are inscribed on the reverse with their original prices of 10, 36, 48, and 66 livres, and six have date letters for 1776 or 1777. Several groups of plaques at these prices are recorded in the Sèvres archives as having been delivered in 1776 and 1777 to Simon Poirier and Dominique Daguerre, Parisian dealers who had a near monopoly on Sèvres plaques. Carlin is known to have worked extensively for them, and they probably commissioned this writing table in 1777 or shortly thereafter. From a distance the plaques appear homogeneous in style; however, painters' marks on the backs distinguish the work of three flower painters active at Sèvres: Jean-Baptiste Tandart (active 1754–1803: the two large oval plaques), Jean-Charles Siou (active 1752–92: the four triangular plaques on the door), and Michel-Gabriel Commelin (active 1768–1802: the left segmental plaque and two triangular plaques at back). The plaques on the frieze on the sides and front are unmarked, but are similar to those by Tandart and can be attributed to him. A similar *bonheur-du-jour* appears in the illustrated inventory of Duke Albert of Saxe-Teschen for the palace of Laeken near Brussels (Metropolitan Museum of Art, New York), one in a series of drawings of furniture with Sèvres plaques probably made for Daguerre as advertisements.

Duveen bought this piece privately from the duchesse de Sesto and sold it to Mrs. Rice in 1912.

Oak veneered with satinwood, tulipwood, and mahogany; gilt-bronze mounts; soft-paste porcelain plaques
Stamp: M CARLIN (partially effaced) with the monogram of the Guild, JME (beneath front rail)
Height 40 9/16″ (103 cm), width 27 9/16″ (70 cm), depth 16 15/16″ (43 cm)
Bequest of Eleanore Elkins Rice. 39-41-7

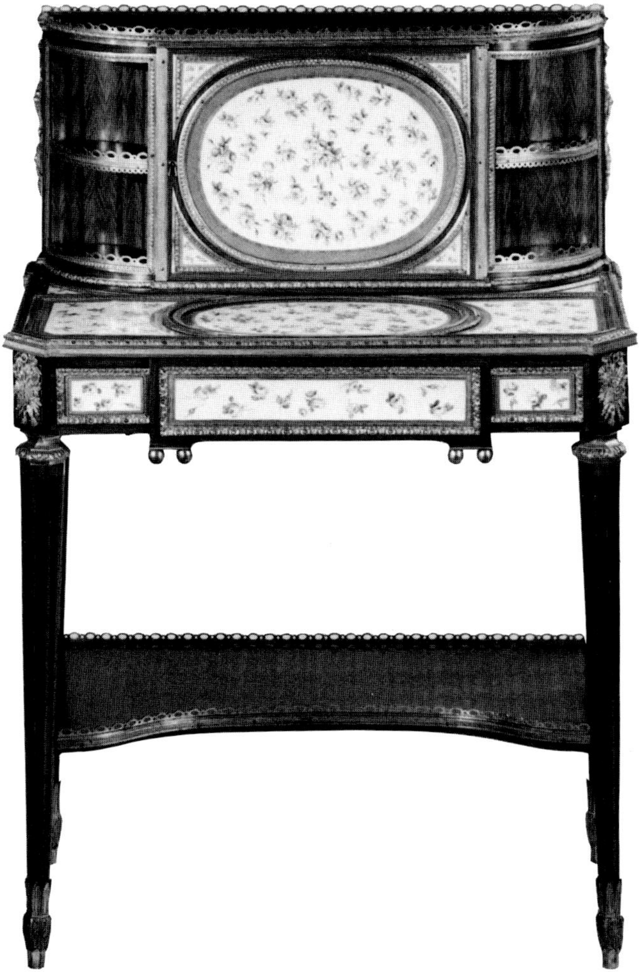

Writing Table, c. 1777–80
Martin Carlin (*maître* 1766, died 1785)

12 This *bonheur-du-jour* and the previous, closely related example are the only known writing tables mounted with this configuration of Sèvres plaques. This table is fitted with fourteen plaques painted with pink roses on a white ground and with turquoise (*bleu céleste*) borders. Eight of these retain original priced factory labels on the reverse and four of the plaques have date letters for 1776. The prices and date correspond with a number of plaques recorded in the Sèvres archives as delivered to the dealers Poirier and Daguerre in the last six months of 1776, and this piece was probably commissioned by them from Carlin at the same time as the previous table, that is, 1777 or shortly thereafter. The plaques are signed by two flower painters who worked at Sèvres: Jean-Baptiste Tandart (active 1754–1803: the four large plaques on the door and tabletop) and Vincent Taillandier (active 1753–90: the two small triangular plaques at back). The plaques on the frieze on the sides and front are unmarked. The drawers of both of the Museum's tables are fitted identically with a hinged writing panel and with compartments for ink and pens. The legs and gilt-bronze mounts on the corners and sides were repeated by Carlin on numerous pieces of furniture.

In the late nineteenth century, this *bonheur-du-jour* was in the collection of Alfred de Rothschild, and it passed on his death in 1918 to Almina, Countess of Carnarvon. It was bought privately from her by Duveen, who clearly foresaw its appeal as the near mate of the *bonheur-du-jour* he had sold to Mrs. Rice in 1912. Mrs. Rice acquired this second *bonheur-du-jour* with Sèvres plaques from Duveen in 1925.

Oak veneered with satinwood, tulipwood, and mahogany; gilt-bronze mounts; soft-paste porcelain plaques
Stamp: M CARLIN with the monogram of the Guild, JME (beneath front rail)

Height 39$\frac{3}{4}$″ (101 cm), width 27$\frac{9}{16}$″ (70 cm), depth 16$\frac{1}{8}$″ (41 cm)
Bequest of Eleanore Elkins Rice. 39-41-6

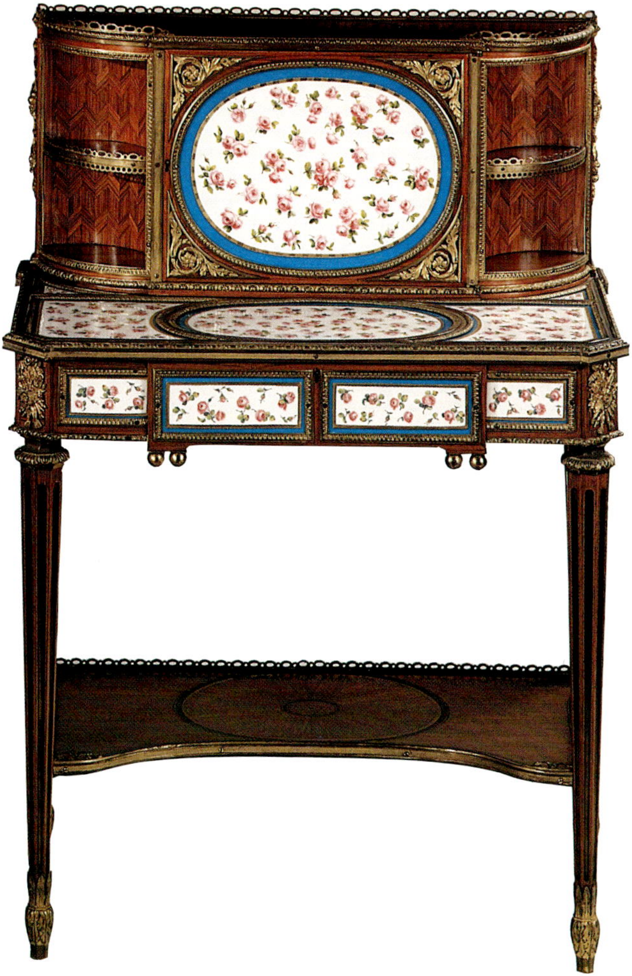

Jardiniere, c. 1776–77
Martin Carlin (*maître* 1766, died 1785)

14

This jardiniere, or plant stand, is fitted with eight porcelain plaques painted with pink roses on a white ground and with turquoise (*bleu céleste*) borders. They are marked on the reverse with the crossed *LL*s of the Sèvres manufactory and the painter's mark, a fleur-de-lis, of Vincent Taillandier, a flower painter who worked at Sèvres from 1753 to 1790. The plaques, of a bowed shape rarely made at Sèvres, fit the jardiniere tightly and were clearly ordered specifically for this use. They retain on the backs the original priced labels of 60 and 72 livres and were probably among the two lots of "plaques bombées" at these prices recorded in the Sèvres archives as delivered in the second half of 1776 to the dealers Poirier and Daguerre, who then commissioned this piece from Carlin.

The jardiniere was inherited in 1918 by Almina, Countess of Carnarvon, from Alfred de Rothschild; it was sold by Duveen to Mrs. Rice in 1923.

Oak veneered with tulipwood, rosewood, and other woods; gilt-bronze mounts; soft-paste porcelain plaques
Stamp: M CARLIN with the monogram of the Guild, JME (on side of removable oak container)
Height 33 7/16″ (85 cm), width 25 15/16″ (66 cm), depth 18½″ (47 cm)
Bequest of Eleanore Elkins Rice. 39-41-13

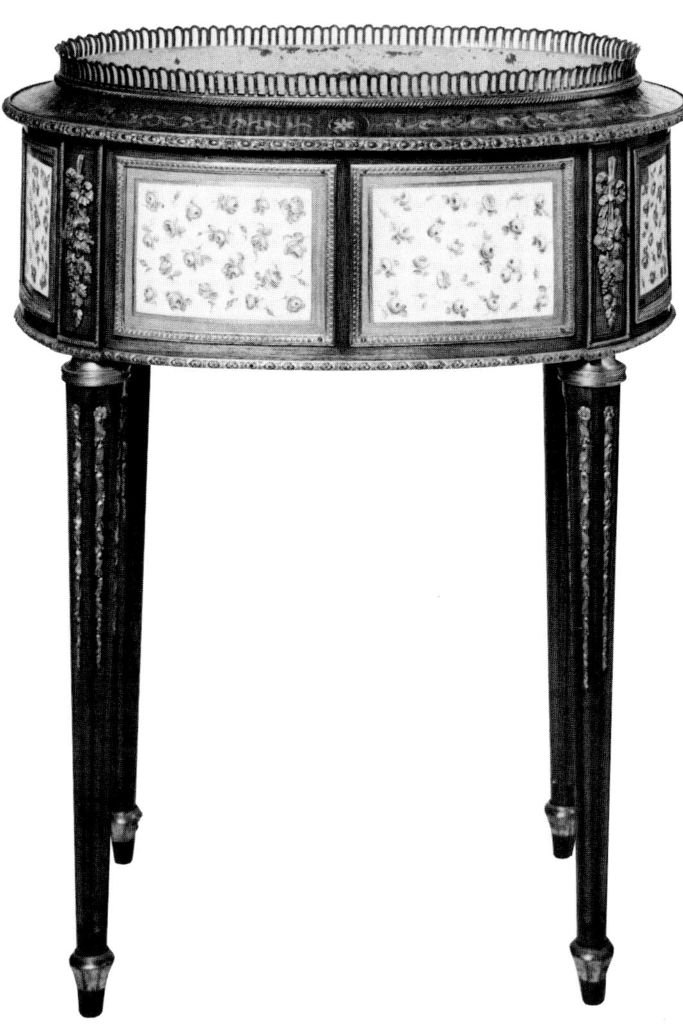

Gueridon Table, c. 1780
Martin Carlin (*maître* 1766, died 1785)

16 Traditionally, a gueridon is a small stand or table used to support a free-standing candlestick or candelabrum, a form known in France since the mid-seventeenth century. The type of gueridon with movable candle arms on an attached adjustable shaft, like this one, came into existence later, by the middle of the eighteenth century. It served as a work or reading table and became known as a *serviteur-fidèle* ("faithful servant"). Carlin produced a number of these tables with each of the tops fitted with a plaque of soft-paste Sèvres porcelain. The plaque on this gueridon is painted with roses on a white ground and a border patterned with gold circles on a violet ground known at Sèvres as *oeil-de-perdrix* ("partridge eye"). It is marked on the reverse with the date letters for 1779 within the crossed *LL*s of the Sèvres factory. Although it is unstamped, a similar gueridon table in the Museum with a Sèvres plaque painted with roses and made in the same year can be attributed to Carlin.

Both tables were formerly in the collection of J. Pierpont Morgan, exhibited at the Metropolitan Museum of Art in 1914, and sold by Duveen to Mrs. Rice the following year.

Oak veneered with tulipwood, satinwood, boxwood, and sycamore, and solid purplewood; gilt-bronze mounts; soft-paste porcelain plaque
Stamp: M CARLIN (partially effaced) (under upper tier)
Height 34⅝″ (88 cm), width 14 9/16″ (37 cm), depth 12″ (30.5 cm)
Bequest of Eleanore Elkins Rice. 39-41-15

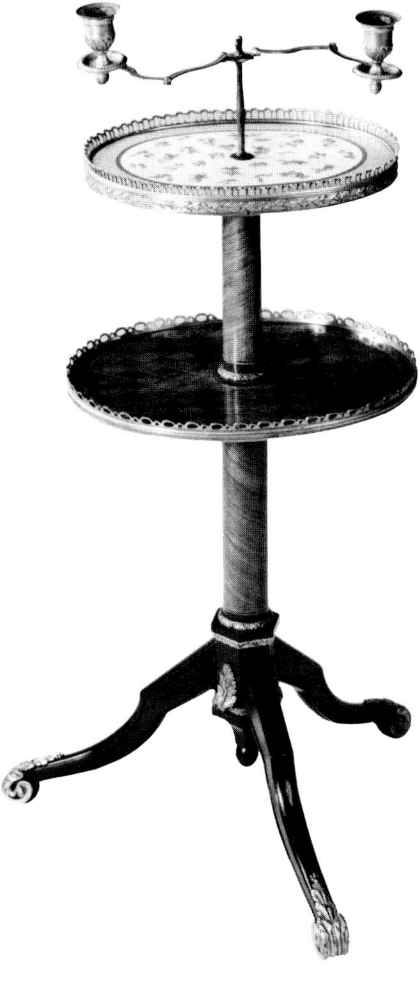

Commode, c. 1770
Martin Carlin (*maître* 1766, died 1785)

The sophisticated veneer on this commode, one of a pair in the collections, extends to the inside of the doors and drawer fronts, and exemplifies Carlin's refined cabinetwork. The principal veneer is holly—an unusual feature on eighteenth-century commodes but not unique in Carlin's work, as another, almost identical pair of commodes by him is known. The trellis marquetry of curvilinear design enclosing quatrefoils appears both in the work of Carlin and in that of other cabinetmakers of this period. The mounts were used again by Carlin on later pieces, most notably the male mask flanked by acanthus leaves on the apron, which reappears on a commode of about 1775 inscribed by the dealer Poirier (ex collection Wildenstein), and on a bookcase of about 1780–85 (Metropolitan Museum of Art, New York). The guilloche mount on the frieze is also repeated on the Poirier commode. The motif of a satyr mask was often incorporated by Carlin into corner mounts (compare the smaller mounts of less dramatic expression on the *bonheur-du-jour* on page 8).

The Museum's commodes were in the collection of Lord Walter Talbot Kerr, at Brocket Hall, Hatfield, the contents of which were sold in London in 1923. Mrs. Rice acquired them from Duveen the following year.

Oak veneered with holly, ebony, and sycamore; gilt-bronze mounts; marble top
Stamp: M CARLIN with the monogram of the Guild, JME (on top of front corners)
Height $35\frac{1}{16}$″ (89 cm), width $66\frac{1}{8}$″ (168 cm), depth $23\frac{5}{8}$″ (60 cm)
Bequest of Eleanore Elkins Rice. 39-41-2

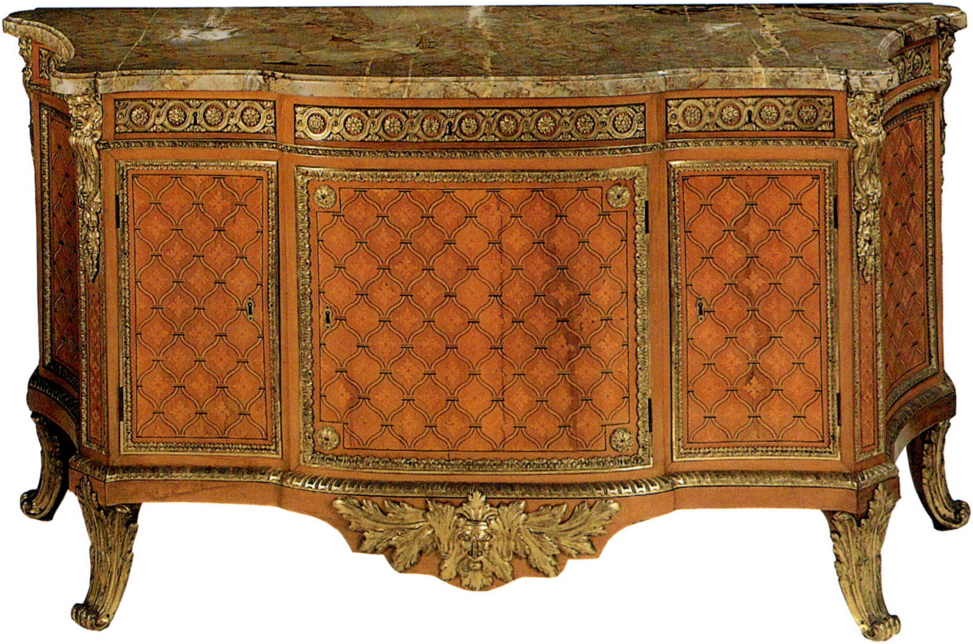

Commode, c. 1780–85
Jean-Henri Riesener (*maître* 1768, died 1806)

20 This commode is similar in shape, marquetry, and mounts to several commodes executed about 1780–85 by Jean-Henri Riesener, the greatest Parisian cabinetmaker of the Louis XVI period. A commode made for Marie Antoinette's Petit Trianon, another for her *cabinet intérieur* at the Tuileries (1784, Louvre, Paris), and two made in 1783 for the apartment at Fontainebleau of the youngest sister of Louis XVI, Mme Elisabeth (Detroit Institute of Arts and private collection, Paris) are all of a similar tripartite form with projecting central panel, incurved splayed sides, and trellis marquetry. The marquetry—diamond-shaped panels of alternating light- and dark-stained sycamore edged with holly and ebony fillets—is the simpler of two patterns used by Riesener, the other, a fret marquetry enclosing water lilies or florets. Both the marquetry and the pierced frieze mount are framed to give the illusion that the central panel is superimposed over the flanking surfaces. The gilt-bronze frieze, corner, escutcheon, apron, and leg mounts reappear in varying combinations on many pieces of furniture by Riesener. They were previously attributed to the bronze worker and gilder Pierre Gouthière, but it is now thought that they were made in Riesener's own workshop. As an *ébéniste ordinaire du Roi,* he was exempt from guild regulation and therefore entitled to produce his own mounts.

Although it closely resembles several royal commodes, this example is without inventory marks and its early history remains unknown. It was acquired by J. Pierpont Morgan in 1906, exhibited with his collection in 1914, and sold by Duveen to Mrs. Rice the following year.

Oak veneered with sycamore, amaranth, ebony, and holly; gilt-bronze mounts; marble top
Height $36\frac{7}{16}$″ (92.5 cm), width $54\frac{1}{2}$″ (138.5 cm), depth $23\frac{13}{16}$″ (60.5 cm)
Bequest of Eleanore Elkins Rice. 39-41-4

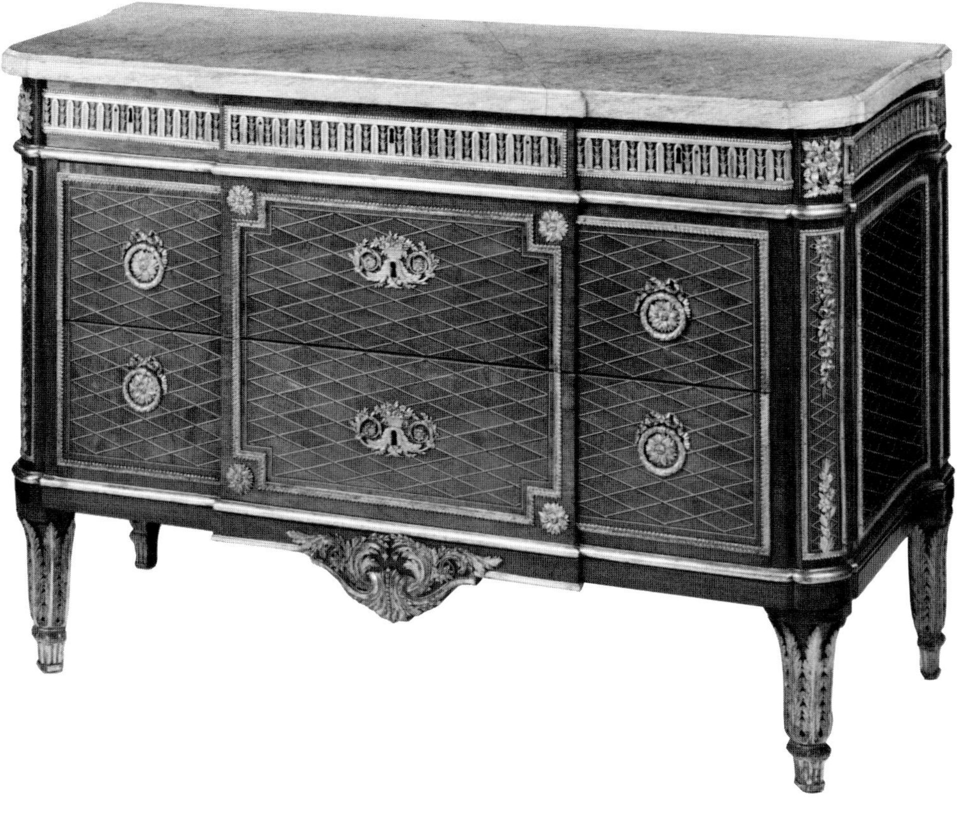

Commode, c. 1790
Attributed to Jean-Henri Riesener (*maître* 1768, died 1806)

Jean-Henri Riesener's workshop in the Louvre produced a large body of furniture, ranging from royal commissions of the highest quality to pieces of a more commercial nature for private clients. This elaborately inlaid commode falls into the latter category and is attributed to Riesener's workshop on the basis of the marquetry (the cornucopias and baskets of fruit and flowers are related to those on a secretary made by Riesener for Marie Antoinette at the château of Saint-Cloud and now in the Frick Collection, New York), the gilt-bronze mounts, and the construction. The stamp DV and the number written on the bottom are yet to be identified.

This commode was exhibited as part of the collection of J. Pierpont Morgan at the Metropolitan Museum of Art in 1914 and was acquired by Mrs. Rice from Duveen the following year.

Oak veneered with mahogany, sycamore, boxwood, and holly; gilt-bronze mounts; Brescia marble top
Stamp: DV (twice on bottom)
Number: 3562 A (in black crayon on bottom of center drawer)
Height 36″ (91.5 cm), width 55″ (139.5 cm), depth 25¾″ (65.5 cm)
Bequest of Eleanore Elkins Rice. 39-41-3

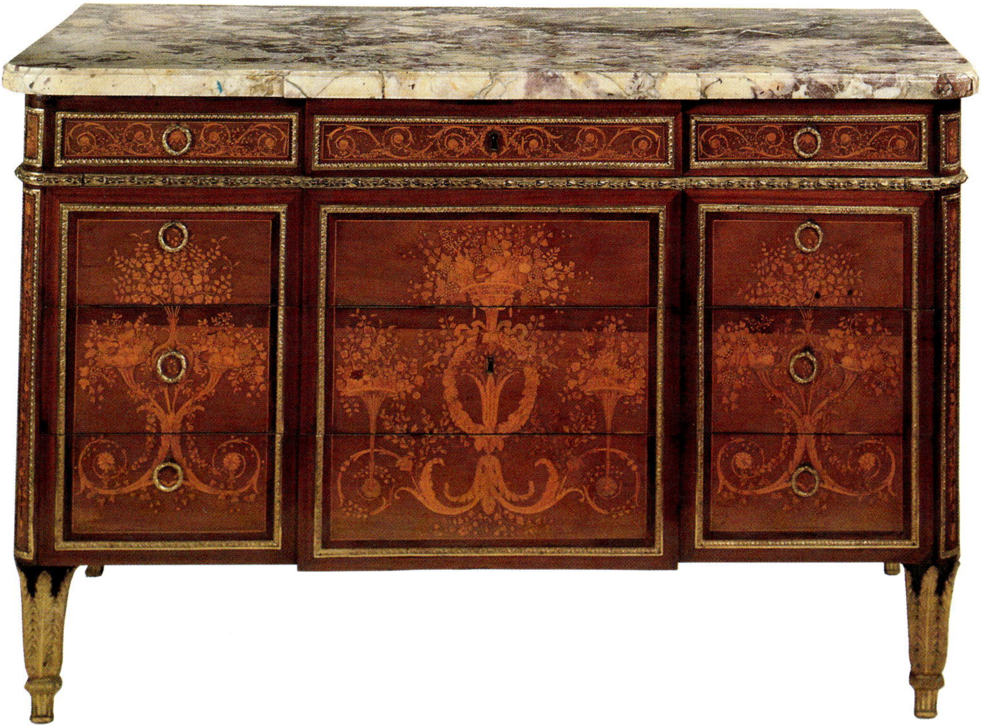

Writing Table, 1783
Jean-Henri Riesener (*maître* 1768, died 1806)

24 Jean-Henri Riesener delivered this table on December 31, 1783, for Mme Elisabeth at Versailles, where she occupied an apartment on the first floor overlooking the orangery. The top is veneered with fret marquetry in a diamond-shaped pattern of ribbons, which break at the crossings into circles and frame a water lily in each compartment. (The scrollwork in the central oval is a later replacement.) The number painted on the underside identifies the entry in the royal furniture inventory, the *Journal du Garde Meuble,* which describes this table in some detail. The writing slide, which pulls out from the front, was originally fitted with gold-tooled black morocco leather, and the writing materials in the right-hand drawer originally consisted of a gilt-copper inkwell, pounce pot, and sponge box. The table also appears in a list of furniture sent from Versailles to the Tuileries in October 1789 as "3306—Une trés belle table qui avait été faite pour la Reine" ("A very beautiful table made for the Queen"). This may have been a case of mistaken numbering, or possibly shows that when it was delivered to Versailles, Marie Antoinette found it to her taste and appropriated it for her own use. The gilt-bronze relief of putti playing musical instruments, which appears on both sides of the table, is found also on two similar tables made by Riesener in 1781 for Marie Antoinette for the châteaux of Versailles and Marly (Metropolitan Museum of Art, New York, and Museu Calouste Gulbenkian, Lisbon). It was often used by Riesener, who varied its length according to the requirements of each piece.

This table is among the several pieces Mrs. Rice acquired from Duveen that had previously been in the collections of Alfred de Rothschild and Almina, Countess of Carnarvon.

Oak veneered with mahogany, satinwood, purplewood, and other woods; gilt-bronze mounts
Number: 3306 (French royal inventory number in black paint on underside)

Height $29\frac{3}{4}$" (75.5 cm), width $33\frac{1}{16}$" (84 cm), depth $19\frac{5}{16}$" (49 cm)
Bequest of Eleanore Elkins Rice. 39-41-9

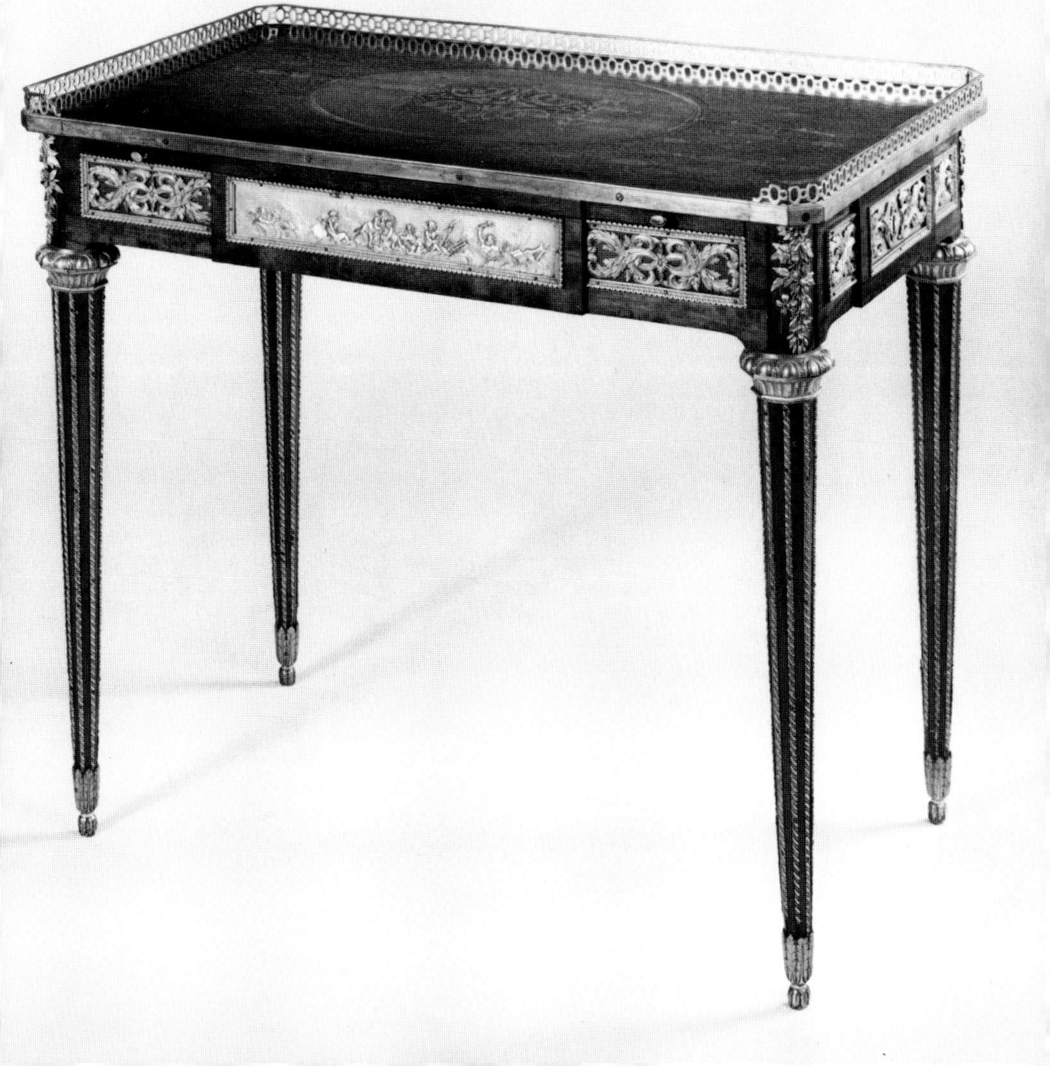

Writing Table, 1783
Jean-Henri Riesener (*maître* 1768, died 1806)

26 This table was delivered on December 31, 1783, by Jean-Henri Riesener for Marie Antoinette at the château of Marly, near Versailles, and is described briefly in the royal furniture inventory, the *Journal du Garde Meuble:* "No 3316—Une table à ecrire de marqueterie . . . Pour la Reine à Marly" ("A marquetry writing table . . . for the Queen at Marly"). The top is veneered with a fret pattern of diamond-shaped panels of alternating light- and dark-stained sycamore edged with boxwood and ebony fillets. This and the previous table made for Mme Elisabeth at Versailles have identical scrollwork in the central ovals, later additions replacing what was probably a floral or emblematic trophy of the type seen on a number of similar tables by Riesener. The gilt-bronze mounts of interlaced acanthus branches encircling rosettes and the paneled legs with twisted-rope moldings in indented corners were used by Riesener on a number of other pieces, the most closely related being a writing table in the Louvre and one in the Rothschild Collection at Waddesdon Manor. This table is fitted with a writing slide, which draws out from the front, and a drawer on each side, the right one originally divided into three compartments for writing materials.

Both of the Museum's tables belonged to Alfred de Rothschild, and descended in 1918 to Almina, Countess of Carnarvon, from whom they were bought by Duveen. The tops may have been altered before the tables entered the Rothschild Collection, or later, possibly by Duveen, in an attempt to relate them more closely. Although they are clearly not a pair, they were sold as such by Duveen to Mrs. Rice in 1925.

Oak veneered with mahogany, sycamore, satinwood, boxwood, ebony, and other woods; gilt-bronze mounts
Stamp: J. H. Riesener (beneath left rail)
Numbers: Du No 3316 (French royal inventory number), M. No 49 (Marly number) (in ink on underside)
Height 28 9/16″ (72.5 cm), width 33 1/4″ (84.5 cm), depth 19 5/16″ (49 cm)
Bequest of Eleanore Elkins Rice. 39-41-8

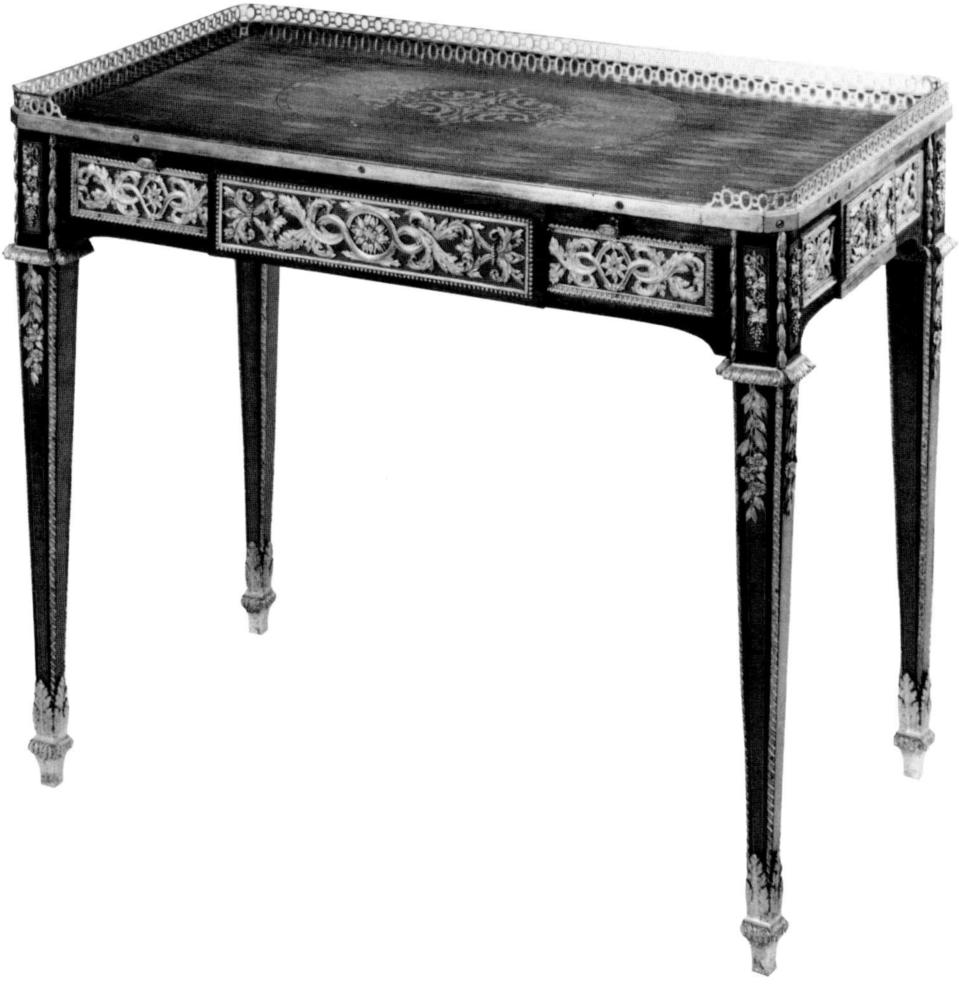

Writing Table, c. 1761–72
Joseph Baumhauer (died 1772)

This writing table is fitted with twenty-four plaques of Sèvres porcelain painted with bunches of flowers within white quatrefoil reserves on a green ground. The crossed *LL*s of the Sèvres factory and an unidentified painter's mark appear on the back of each plaque. The table is one of four nearly identical pieces produced by the *ébéniste privilégié du Roi* Joseph Baumhauer between about 1761 and 1772 (the others at Waddesdon Manor, Boughton House, and in the Lehman Collection at the Metropolitan Museum of Art, where the Sèvres plaques have been replaced with marquetry). The plaques on the Museum's table are not dated, whereas those on the Waddesdon and Boughton tables have date marks for 1760 and 1761. These tables may all have been commissioned by the dealer Simon Poirier, who bought Sèvres plaques from the factory at a discount and ordered furniture to incorporate them, principally from Joseph Baumhauer, Martin Carlin, Roger Vandercruse (known as Lacroix), and Bernard II Van Risamburgh. A commode by Van Risamburgh mounted with ninety plaques and sold by Poirier to the prince de Condé (private collection, Paris) is the most famous piece of this type. Baumhauer also made similar writing tables without Sèvres plaques, of which the finest example known is a table with black Japanese lacquer in the Louvre (Grog Collection).

This writing table was in the collection of Viscount Clifden and then owned by the financier and railroad executive George Jay Gould before it was sold to Mrs. Rice by Duveen in 1925.

Oak veneered with tulipwood; gilt-bronze mounts; soft-paste porcelain plaques; morocco leather
Height 30 5/16″ (77 cm), width 45 1/4″ (115 cm), depth 23 1/4″ (59 cm)
Bequest of Eleanore Elkins Rice. 39-41-10

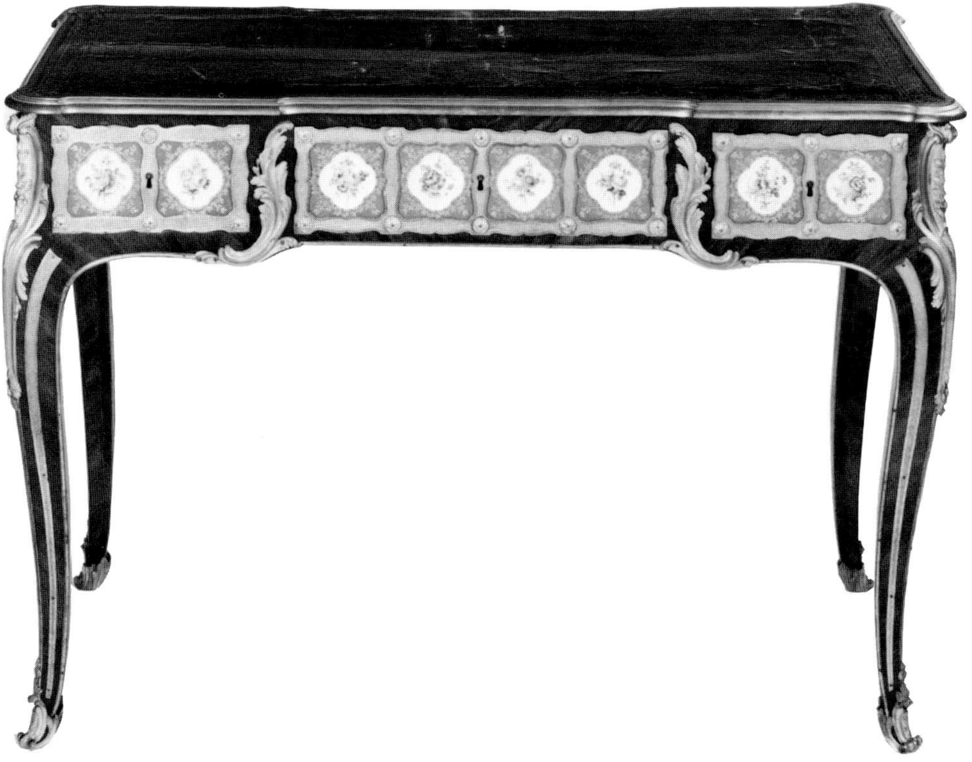

Drop-Front Secretary, c. 1790
Attributed to Adam Weisweiler (*maître* 1778, died 1820)

30 Adam Weisweiler produced highly finished furniture in a distinctive style, often characterized by a light, almost fragile appearance. Among the features on this secretary (one of a pair in the Museum) that are typical of his work are the elaborate gilt-bronze columns of twisted and fluted design set into the recesses of the front corners and the thin, octagonal, tapered legs with peg-top feet connected by interlaced curving stretchers. The finely chased gilt bronze may be the work of Pierre Gouthière, with whom Weisweiler is thought to have collaborated on some of his pre-Revolutionary commissions. The strongly mottled veneer is of thuja, a wood native to Africa and often used by Weisweiler. The oval pictorial porcelain plaque set into the drop front was made at Sèvres and probably supplied by the dealer Dominique Daguerre, for whom Weisweiler worked extensively. This and the one on the companion piece are copied from paintings by François Desportes (1661–1743), which were purchased for the Sèvres factory in 1784. Large plaques of this type were rare in the late eighteenth century. Weisweiler used two similar plaques painted by Jacques-François Micaud in 1787 on a pair of closely related secretaries in the château of Versailles.

The Museum's secretaries were owned by J. Pierpont Morgan, exhibited in 1914, and sold by Duveen to Mrs. Rice in 1915.

Oak veneered with thuja (exterior) and satinwood (interior); gilt-bronze mounts; soft-paste porcelain plaque; marble top
Stamps: HT (unidentified stamp, twice on top of case); A B DANIELL & SONS, WIGMORE ST. LONDON (dealer's stamp, five times on top of case)
Height 48¾″ (123.5 cm), width 28″ (71 cm), depth 14⅜″ (36.5 cm)
Bequest of Eleanore Elkins Rice. 39-41-5

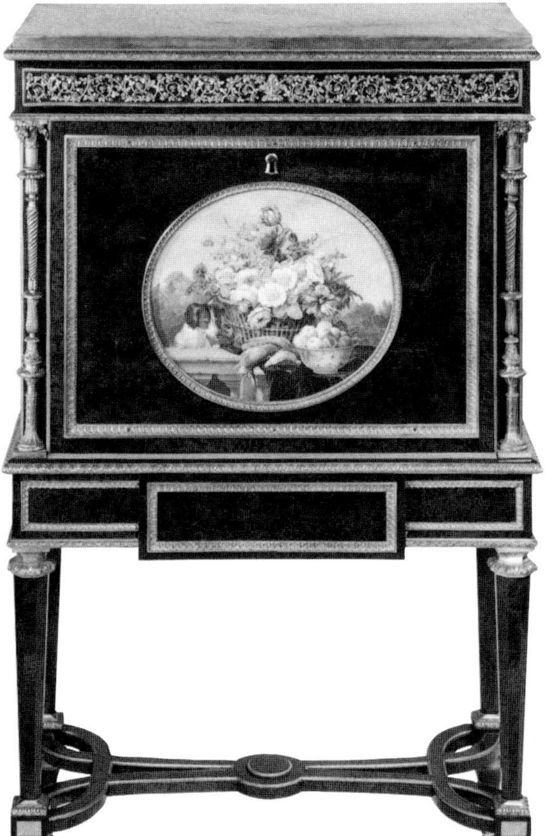

Double Saltcellar, 1757–58
Antoine-Sébastien Durand (active 1740–c. 1785)

32 A reclining infant playing with a ribbon and flanked by stylized seashells designed to hold salt and pepper is placed on asymmetrically disposed foliage, which spills over the edge of the base. The pouting infant is of a type that appears elsewhere in the work of Antoine-Sébastien Durand, a highly regarded silversmith who worked in Paris from 1740 until about 1785. This double saltcellar and its pair in the Louvre are part of a table service including wine coolers and tureens and covers made by two other well-known silversmiths Thomas Germain (died 1748) and Edmé-Pierre Balzac (active 1739—about 1776). Known as the "Orléans Service," it appears to have been assembled gradually by the duc de Penthièvre (1725–1793), descended to his daughter, the duchesse d'Orléans (1753–1821), and then to Louis Philippe (1773–1850), who as the duc d'Orléans put his own coat of arms on all the pieces in the early nineteenth century (he became King of the French in 1830).

The service was dispersed after the First World War and most of the pieces are now in French and American public and private collections.

Silver
Marks: Maker's mark, Paris charge mark for large works 1756–62, Paris warden's mark for 1757–58

Height 4¼″ (10.6 cm)
Purchased. 46-26-1

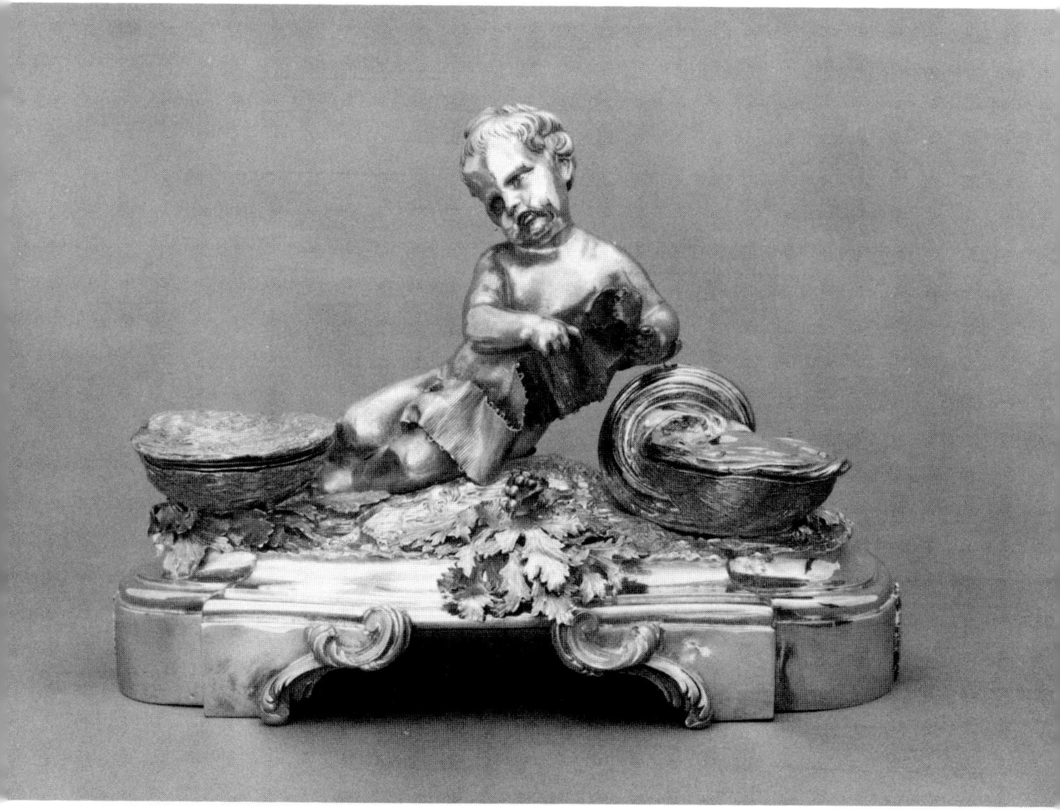

Soup Tureen, Cover, and Stand, 1759
François-Thomas Germain (1726–1791)

This large silver-gilt tureen belonged to an extensive table service, called the "Service de Paris," ordered by the Empress Elizabeth of Russia from François-Thomas Germain in 1756 and completed in 1761. It arrived in St. Petersburg in 1762, the year of Elizabeth's death, but was not delivered to her successor, Catherine the Great, until 1767. The original service included 8 tureens, 120 plates, 96 knives, forks, and spoons, many dishes and covers, 4 pairs of candelabra, 4 ice pails, and numerous smaller pieces. The service was later enlarged with pieces made *en suite* in Russia. The tureens are a tour de force of rococo design. The finely modeled handles are shaped like infant fauns holding swags of drapery, while the detachable finial on the cover is in the form of a putto holding a hawk, with a duck and crane at his feet. On both sides are the cast and applied Russian imperial arms surmounted by the imperial crown. François-Thomas Germain, son of the equally famous goldsmith Thomas Germain (died 1748), was made *orfèvre du Roi* in 1748. He produced enormous quantities of silver in the high rococo style until 1765, when he was declared bankrupt and expelled from his apartments in the Louvre.

This tureen was sold by the Russian government in 1930 and acquired by the Museum in 1954. Others from the service are in The Hermitage, Leningrad, the Museu Calouste Gulbenkian, Lisbon, the Thyssen-Bornemisza Collection, Lugano, and the Museo Nacional de Arte Decorativo, Buenos Aires; a pair of candelabra from the service is in the Cleveland Museum of Art.

Silver gilt
Inscription: Fait par F-T Germain Sculpt^{r} et Orf^{re} du Roy aux Galleries du Louvre à Paris, 1759
Marks: Maker's mark, Paris charge mark for large works 1756–62, Paris warden's mark for 1758–59, discharge mark for export work 1733[?]–75, St. Petersburg mark of 1762 with controller's mark and 90 [for 90% purity] (on tureen and stand)
Height 17″ (43.1 cm)
Purchased. 54-81-1a,b,c

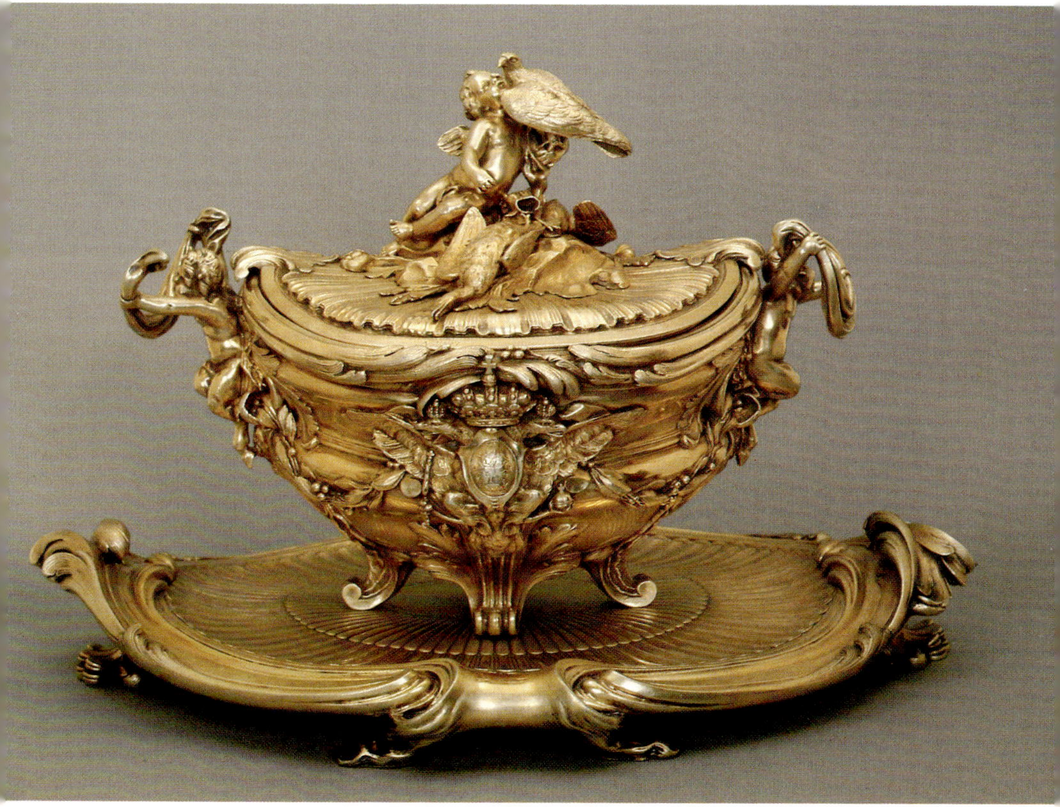

Clock, c. 1750
Jean-Joseph de Saint-Germain (active 1747–72)

36 Jean-Joseph de Saint-Germain was a Parisian bronze worker who specialized in clock cases. Three clocks signed by him are in the Louvre in Paris and others are in the Amalienborg Palace, Copenhagen; Fitzwilliam Museum, Cambridge; Metropolitan Museum of Art, New York; and J. Paul Getty Museum, Malibu. This gilt-bronze case with a winged dragon and putto is the only known version that Saint-Germain made of this clock. Little is known about the maker of the works, Jean-Baptiste-Charles Paillard (*maître* 1750), who was a member of a large Parisian family of clockmakers. Although the placement of the winding holes close to the rim is an unusual feature, the movement and dial appear to be original.

Gilt bronze and enamel
Stamp: S^{T} GERMAIN (on base at back)
Signature: J.B. Paillard Paris (on works)
Height 24″ (61 cm)

Gift of Mr. and Mrs. Rodolphe Meyer de Schauensee. 51-32-1

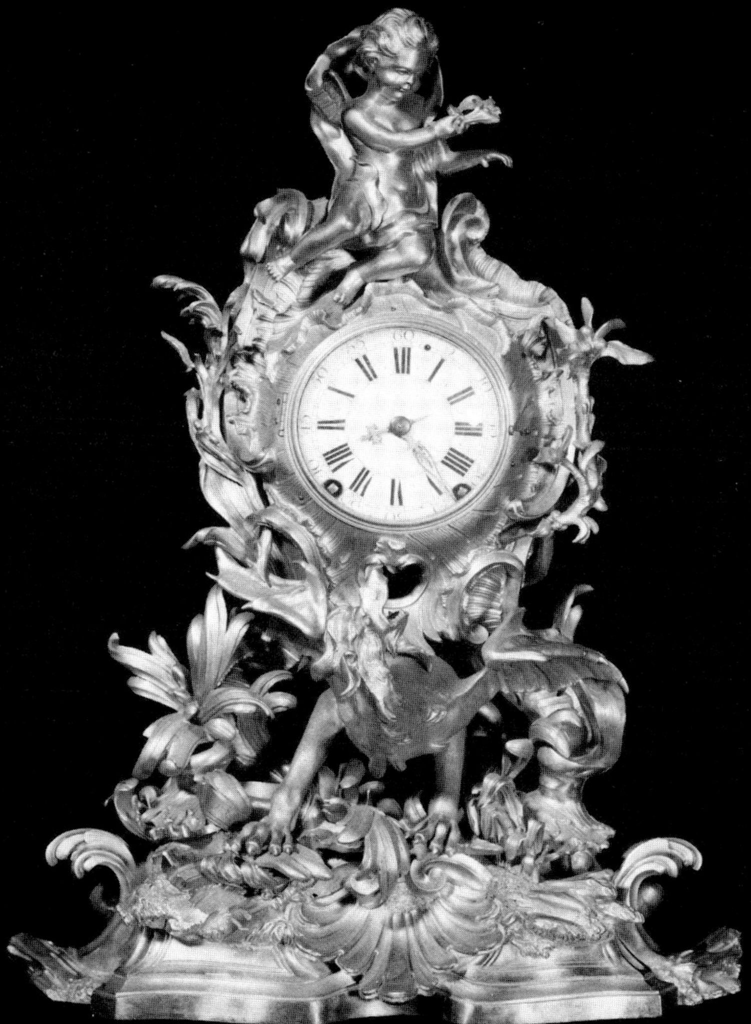

Clock, c. 1780

38 This clock presents an allegory of love and friendship. The female figure is a portrait of Mme de Pompadour, Louis XV's mistress, as a deity or priestess of Friendship. In her right hand she holds two hearts, while her left hand supports an oval enamel plaque, which rests on a truncated column of blue and white Sèvres porcelain. Around the dial of the clock is a beribboned wreath made of roses and bay leaves. The gilt-bronze base of the column is chased with forget-me-nots, which are repeated amid the swags of laurel leaves in the panels on the marble base. On the right side, a child plays with a dog (Mme de Pompadour had two pet dogs, Constance and Fidélité). The enamel plaque, which repeats in miniature the allegorical and symbolical themes, depicts two burning hearts on an altar, a cupid wreathing it with a garland of roses, and another cupid and a dog at one side. The sanctuary is decorated with swags of laurel and at the top, a scroll is inscribed "L'AMITIÉ LES UNIT" ("Friendship unites these two hearts"). The conciliation of love and friendship was a popular rococo theme; in this case the reference is specifically to the affair between Mme de Pompadour and Louis XV, which she had tried to end amicably in 1753. The design is based on a statue of Mme de Pompadour as Friendship, executed by Jean-Baptiste Pigalle and installed at Versailles in 1753, and on a series of etchings by her begun the same year. Versions of this clock are at Versailles and in the Metropolitan Museum of Art, New York, Museum of Fine Arts, Boston, and Walters Art Gallery, Baltimore. The signature on the movement is for Jean-Louis Montjoye, who is recorded in Paris from 1772 until after 1781. The model may have been available from the dealer Daguerre, for a drawing of it belongs to the series apparently made for him as advertisements (Metropolitan Museum of Art).

Gilt bronze, enamel, marble, and
hard-paste porcelain
Signature: L. Montjoye Paris (on dial)
Height 13" (33.1 cm)
Bequest of Eleanore Elkins Rice. 39-41-58

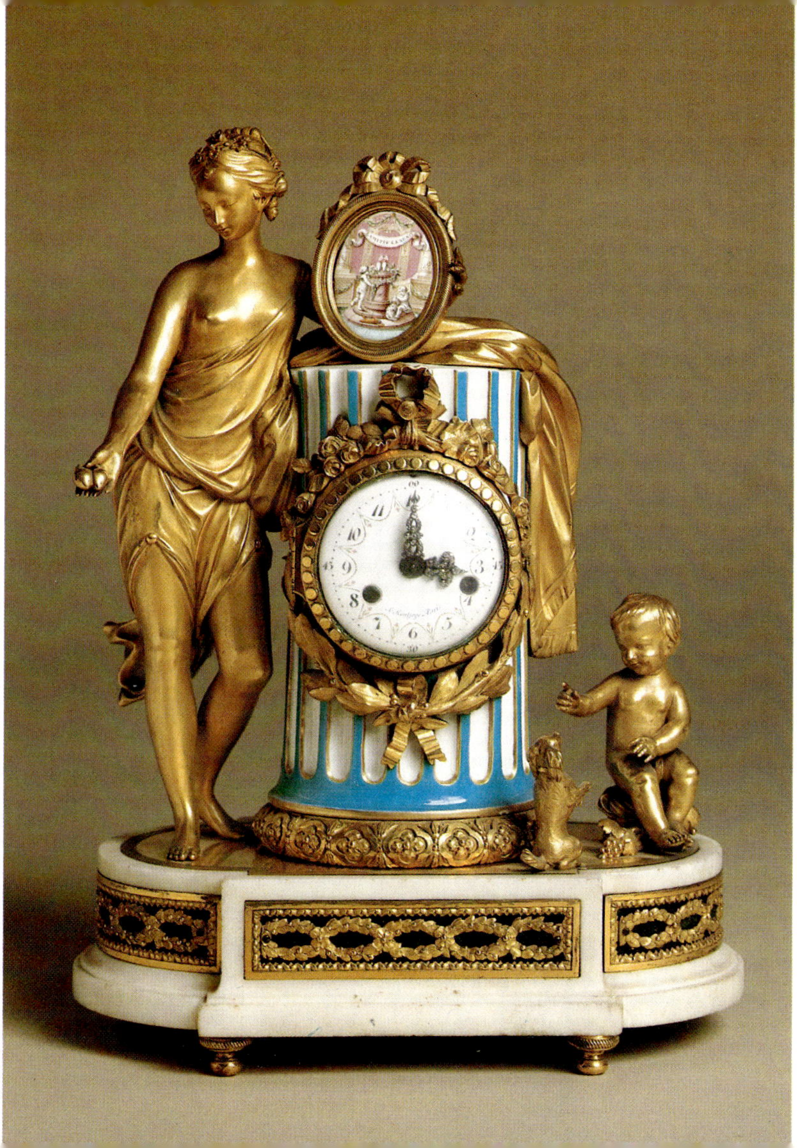

Vase, 1768–69
Manufacture Royale de Porcelaine, Sèvres

40 This vase, one of a pair in the Museum, is painted with a dark-blue ground, a color known in the early records of the Sèvres factory as *bleu nouveau.* It is decorated with six profile heads, painted in grisaille on brown ovals, beneath gold oak leaves and bows of ribbon and separated by three vertical gold bands suggesting triglyphs from a Doric frieze. The simulated-marble medallion portraits, which were introduced at the Sèvres factory in 1768, have been attributed to Jean-Baptiste-Etienne Genest (active 1752–89). As head of the painters' workshop, he decorated some of the most important pieces of Sèvres porcelain, including a number of plates for the famous dinner service ordered by Catherine the Great of Russia. Five pairs of vases of this model, known at Sèvres as "Vase Carrache" (the origin of which is unclear), have been documented—a pair in the Detroit Institute of Arts, another in the Victoria and Albert Museum, London, and two pairs at Waddesdon Manor.

The Museum's vases were sold to Mrs. Rice by Duveen in 1925 along with an extensive group of Sèvres porcelain.

Hard-paste porcelain painted with
enamel colors and gilt
Height 23¾" (60.3 cm)
Bequest of Eleanore Elkins Rice. 39-41-36

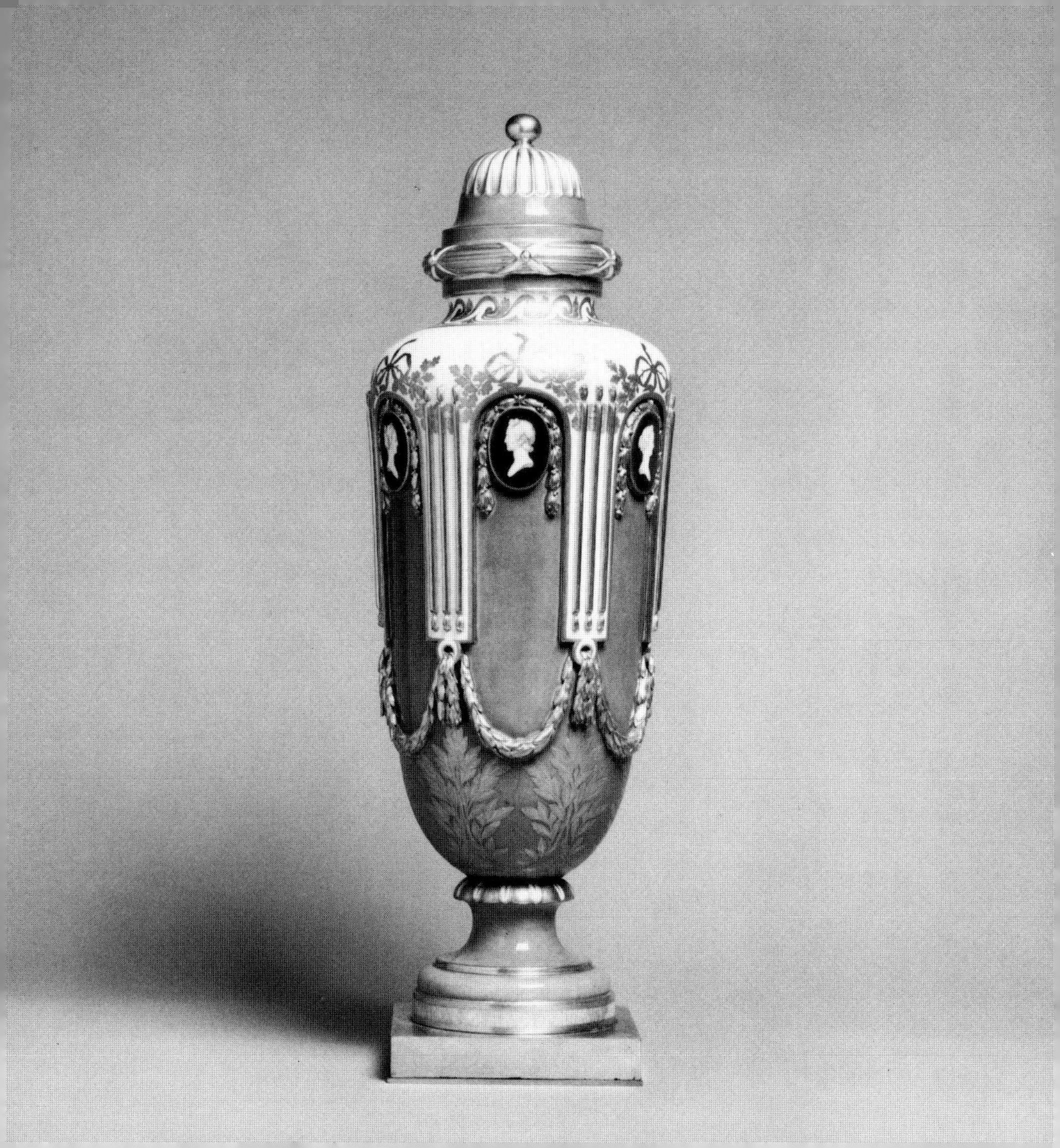

Firedog, c. 1775–80
Pierre Gouthière (1732–1814)

42 On this firedog, one of a pair, a bronze eagle with wings spread holds down a salamander with one claw and the thunderbolts of Jupiter with the other. The firedogs, which originally displayed the cipher of the duchesse de Mazarin in the wreaths on the gilt-bronze bases, were twice offered for sale from her collection (December 10, 1781, and July 27, 1784) as the work of Pierre Gouthière, the most famous bronze worker and gilder of the Louis XVI period. The firedogs later entered the collection of the comte de Vaudreuil and in the 1840s belonged to Lady Blessington at Gore House, London, where they were said to have been acquired from the château of Malmaison. In the Gore House sale of 1849, they were bought by one of the greatest collectors of the nineteenth century, the fourth Marquess of Hertford, who was then restoring as a second residence, the château of Bagatelle in the Bois de Boulogne, Paris. The Bagatelle had been reconstructed in 1777 by François-Joseph Belanger for the comte d'Artois (later Charles X), with chimneypieces by Gouthière and his assistants. In bringing the firedogs to Bagatelle, Lord Hertford integrated works by Gouthière in a manner rarely achieved in the nineteenth century. They descended to Victoria, Lady Sackville, who in 1913 sold them to the Paris art dealer Jacques Seligmann. Duveen sold them to Mrs. Rice in 1925 as the work of Gouthière, although they were not clearly documented as such until 1953 by the Museum's director Fiske Kimball. Despite Gouthière's eminence, the number of his documented and securely attributed works is small.

Patinated bronze, gilt-bronze base
Height 17¾″ (45 cm)
Bequest of Eleanore Elkins Rice
39-41-25a

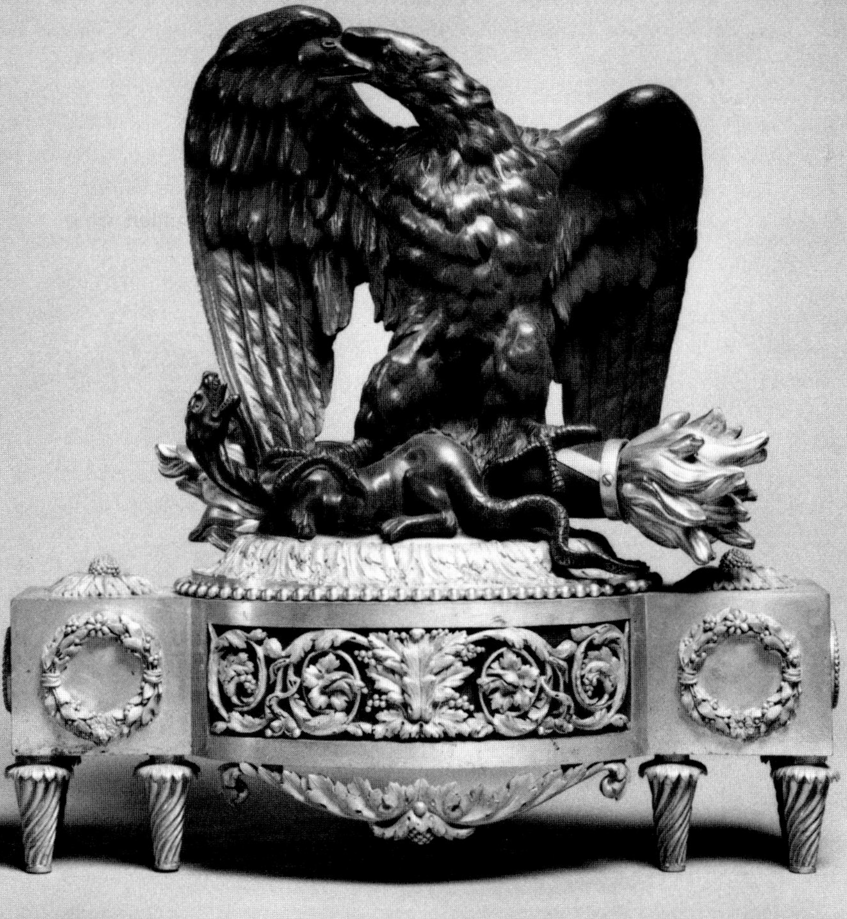

Wall Light, 1784

44 Eight wall lights were delivered in August 1784 to Louis XVI's aunts, Mesdames Victoire, Adélaïde, and Sophie (Mesdames Tantes, as the elderly spinster princesses were known), for the Grand Salon of the château of Bellevue, located between Meudon and Saint-Cloud near Paris. The château was built in 1748 by Louis XV as a country house for Mme de Pompadour and subsequently passed to his daughters, the three princesses. They left Bellevue in 1791 and it was largely demolished in 1823. Four of the wall lights are in the Philadelphia Museum of Art and the other four are in a private collection in Paris. They were provided by the firm of Darnault, Frères, *Marchands et Miroitiers Ordinaire du Roy,* which specialized in mirrors, veneered furniture, porcelain, chandeliers, wall lights, and bronzes. The wall lights appear in the 1787 inventory of the château, which specifies that the eagles' beaks originally held a gold chain suspended in a figure eight. A pair of mounted celadon vases in the Louvre, delivered to Bellevue by Darnault in June 1785, was probably intended to be *en suite* with the wall lights. Two pairs of gilt-bronze and blued-metal candelabra (one in the J. Paul Getty Museum, Malibu) that show a similar disposition of branches, eagles' heads, and a tripod with flame may also have been made *en suite,* but remain undocumented.

In the late nineteenth century, the wall lights were in the collection of Count Cheremeteff in St. Petersburg. The four examples in Philadelphia were sold to Mrs. Rice by Duveen in 1927.

Gilt bronze
Height 15³⁄₁₆″ (38.6 cm)
Bequest of Eleanore Elkins Rice. 39-41-28a

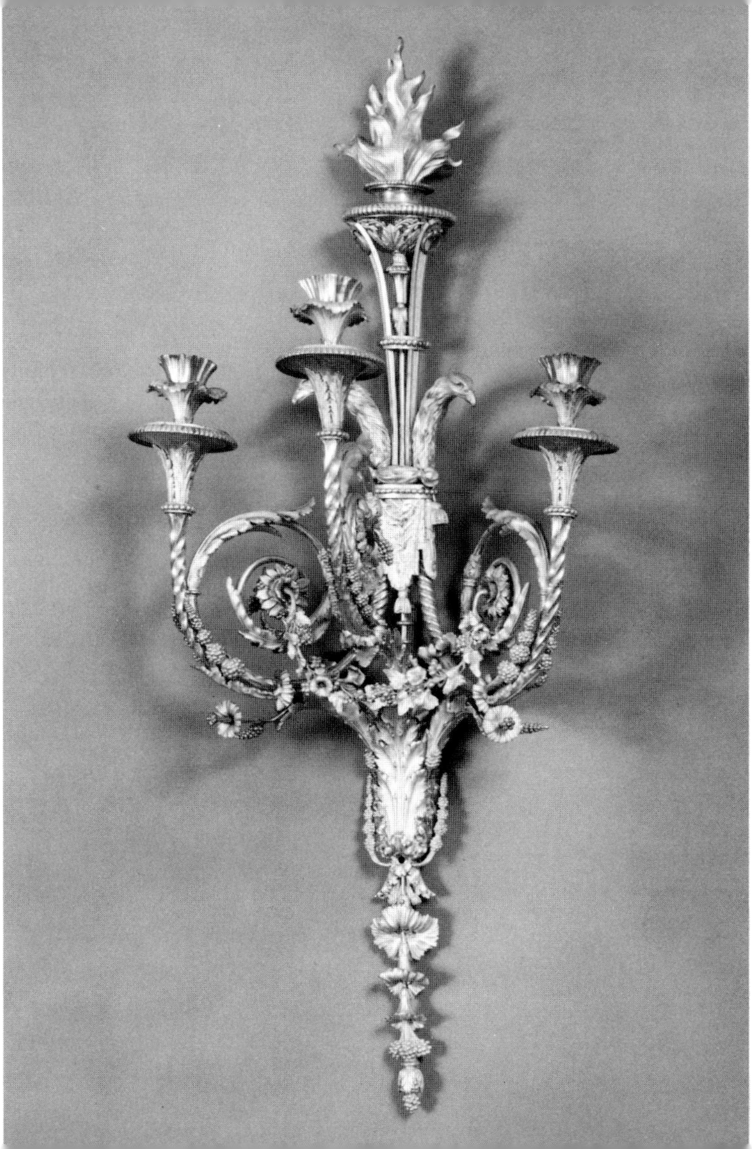

The Basket Weavers, 1741–42
Manufacture Royale de Tapisseries, Beauvais

46 "The Story of Psyche" tapestry series was commissioned by Louis XV from the royal tapestry manufactory at Beauvais in 1737, and was one of the six series designed by François Boucher (1703–1777) during the two decades of his association with Beauvais. Six complete sets of "The Story of Psyche," composed of five tapestries each, were woven between 1741 and 1770, of which the set in the Museum, made for the city of Marseilles and completed in 1742, was the first. The story of Cupid and Psyche derives from the *Metamorphoses* or *Golden Ass* of Apuleius, a Latin romance of the mid-second century A.D. The episodes depicted are the Arrival of Psyche at Cupid's Palace—led by Zephyr, god of the West Wind; the Toilet of Psyche—Psyche surrounded by nymphs; the Riches—Psyche displaying the palace treasures to her sisters; the Abandonment of Psyche by Cupid; and the Basket Weavers—Psyche, in search of her husband, welcomed by a shepherd-philosophe and his daughters, basket weavers. Boucher's complex literary and artistic sources have been traced in the work of the critic and connoisseur Louis Petit de Bachaumont, the paintings of Charles Natoire, and the seventeenth-century versions of the Psyche myth by La Fontaine and Molière.

This set of tapestries was owned in the nineteenth century by the fourth Marquess of Hertford. It passed by descent to Victoria, Lady Sackville, who sold it in 1914 to the Paris firm of Jacques Seligmann, from whom Mrs. Rice acquired it in the early 1920s.

Wool and silk
Signature: F Boucher
9′ 10″ x 7′ 6″ (3 x 2.29 m)
Bequest of Eleanore Elkins Rice. 39-41-30c

For Further Reading

Geoffrey de Bellaigue. *The James A. de Rothschild Collection at Waddesdon Manor: Furniture, Clocks and Gilt Bronzes.* Fribourg, 1974.

Les Ebénistes du XVIIIe siècle français. (Collection Connaissance des Arts "Grands Artisans d'Autrefois.") Pref. by Pierre Verlet. Paris, 1963.

Svend Eriksen. *Early Neo-Classicism in France.* London, 1974.

Comte François de Salverte. *Les Ebénistes du XVIIIe siècle.* 5th ed. rev. Paris, 1962.

Pierre Verlet. *Les Meubles français de XVIIIe siècle: II, Ebénisterie.* Paris, 1956.

Pierre Verlet. *French Royal Furniture.* London, 1963.

Pierre Verlet. *La Maison du XVIIIe siècle en France.* Fribourg, 1966.

F.J.B. Watson. *Wallace Collection Catalogues: Furniture.* London, 1956.

F.J.B. Watson. *Louis XVI Furniture.* New York, 1960.

F.J.B. Watson. *The Wrightsman Collection.* 3 vols. New York, 1966–70.

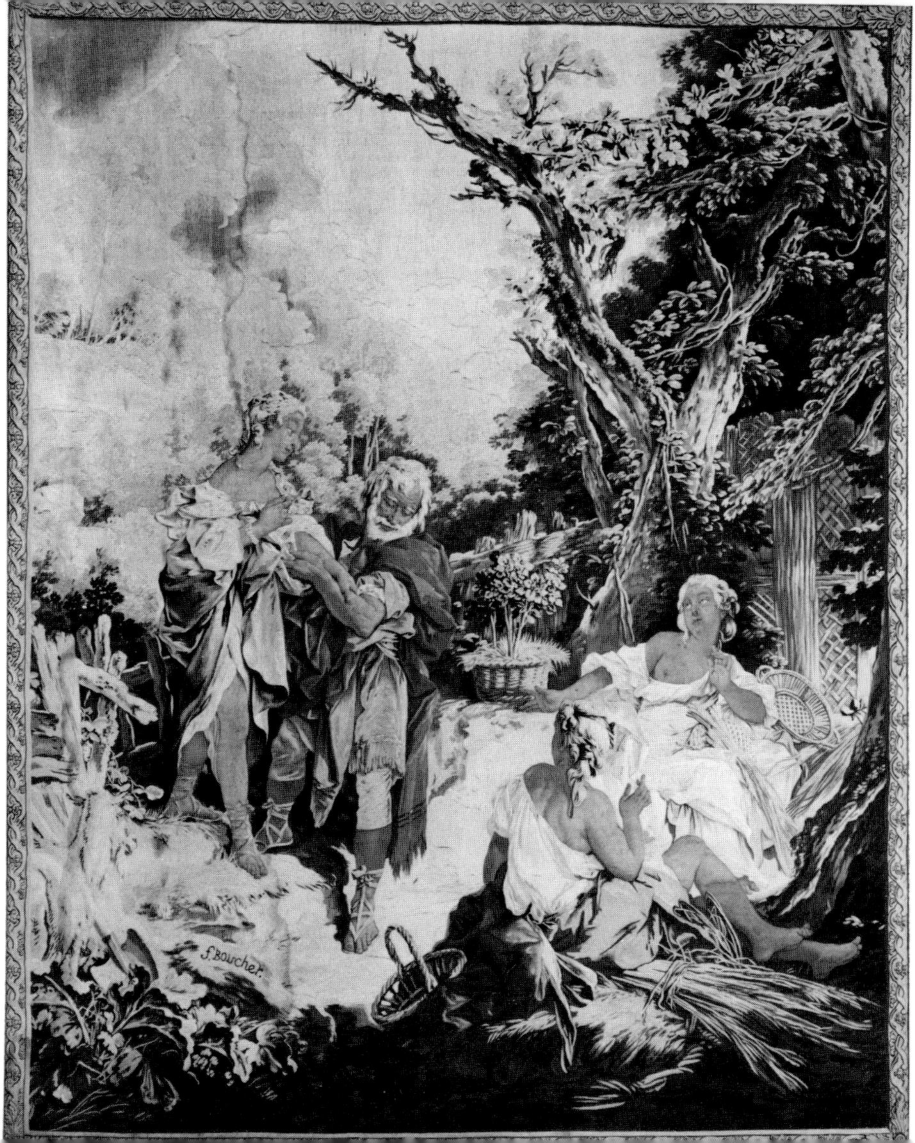
f.Boucher